dashing doggie duds

What lucky dogs! Their owners know that any true fashion hound would trade a favorite bone for one of these swanky crocheted sweaters. The sizes range from small to extra-large, fitting chest sizes up to 24". Perhaps your precious pup would look fetching in her own golden "fleece"? For Independence Day, your canine companion will be proudly patriotic in a crocheted coat of red, white, and blue. And since your four-legged friend is the smartest dog in the world, he won't be surprised to see how quickly you crochet the Santa's helper sweater. From a laid-back camouflage cover to a warm poncho with matching blanket, there's a sweater in this tail-wagging collection that's "paws-itively" perfect for your best little buddy.

LEISURE ARTS, INC.
Little Rock, Arkansas

1. Pedigreed Poncho

EASY

Shown on Front Cover & page 13.

Size	**Chest Measurement**
Small	16" (40.5 cm)
Medium	20" (51 cm)
Large	24" (61 cm)

Size Note: Instructions are written for size Small with sizes Medium and Large in braces { }. Instructions will be easier to read if you circle all the numbers pertaining to your dog's size. If only one number is given, it applies to all sizes.

MATERIALS

Bulky Weight Yarn 

[6 ounces, 185 yards (170 grams, 169 meters) per skein]: 1 skein

Crochet hook, size K (6.5 mm) **or** size needed for gauge

GAUGE: In pattern, 8 dc = $3^1/_2$" (9 cm);
5 rows = $3^1/_2$" (9 cm)

Gauge Swatch: $4^1/_4$"w x $3^1/_2$"h (10.75 cm x 9 cm)
Ch 13.
Row 1: Dc in fourth ch from hook **(3 skipped chs counts as first dc)** and in each ch across: 11 dc.
Row 2: Ch 3 **(counts as first dc, now and throughout)**, turn; (skip next dc, 2 dc in next dc) 4 times, skip next dc, dc in last dc: 10 dc.
Row 3: Ch 3, turn; dc in same st, ★ skip next 2 dc, 2 dc in sp **before** next dc *(Fig. 4, page 19)*; repeat from ★ 3 times **more**, dc in last dc: 11 dc.
Row 4: Ch 3, turn; (skip next 2 dc, 2 dc in sp **before** next dc) 4 times, skip next dc, dc in last dc: 10 dc.
Row 5: Ch 3, turn; dc in same st, ★ skip next 2 dc, 2 dc in sp **before** next dc; repeat from ★ 3 times **more**, dc in last dc; finish off: 11 dc.

PONCHO
RIBBING

Ch 7{9-11}.

Row 1: Sc in second ch from hook and in each ch across: 6{8-10} sc.

Rows 2 thru 18{22-26}: Ch 1, turn; sc in Back Loop Only of each sc across *(Fig. 1, page 18)*.

Joining Rnd: Ch 1, turn; working in Back Loops Only of sc on last row **and** in free loops of beginning ch *(Fig. 3, page 19)*, slip st in each st across; do **not** finish off.

BODY

Rnd 1 (Right side)**:** Ch 3 **(counts as first dc, now and throughout)**, do **not** turn; work 19{23-27} dc evenly spaced in end of rows around; join with slip st to first dc: 20{24-28} dc.

Rnd 2: Ch 3, do **not** turn; dc in same st, (skip next dc, 2 dc in next dc) 3{4-5} times, skip next dc, (2 dc, ch 2, 2 dc) in next dc, (skip next dc, 2 dc in next dc) 4{5-6} times, skip next dc, (2 dc, ch 2, 2 dc) in next dc, skip last dc; join with slip st to first dc: 24{28-32} dc and 2 ch-2 sps.

Rnd 3: Turn; slip st in sp **before** next dc *(Fig. 4, page 19)*, ch 3, dc in same sp, skip next 2 dc, (2 dc, ch 2, 2 dc) in next ch-2 sp, (skip next 2 dc, 2 dc in sp **before** next dc) across to next ch-2 sp, (2 dc, ch 2, 2 dc) in ch-2 sp, (skip next 2 dc, 2 dc in sp **before** next dc) across; join with slip st to first dc: 28{32-36} dc and 2 ch-2 sps.

Rnds 4 thru 7{9-11}: Turn; slip st in sp **before** next dc, ch 3, dc in same sp, (skip next 2 dc, 2 dc in sp **before** next dc) across to next ch-2 sp, (2 dc, ch 2, 2 dc) in ch-2 sp, (skip next 2 dc, 2 dc in sp **before** next dc) across to next ch-2 sp, (2 dc, ch 2, 2 dc) in ch-2 sp, (skip next 2 dc, 2 dc in sp **before** next dc) across; join with slip st to first dc: 44{56-68} dc and 2 ch-2 sps.

EDGING

Sizes Small and Large Only

Turn; slip st in sp **before** next dc, ch 3, 4 dc in same sp, (skip next 2 dc, sc in sp **before** next dc, skip next 2 dc, 5 dc in sp **before** next dc) across to within 2 dc of next ch-2 sp, skip next dc, sc in next dc, 5 dc in ch-2 sp, sc in next dc, skip next dc, 5 dc in sp **before** next dc, skip next 2 dc, sc in sp **before** next dc, (skip next 2 dc, 5 dc in sp **before** next dc, skip next 2 dc, sc in sp **before** next dc) across to next ch-2 sp, 5 dc in ch-2 sp, skip next 2 dc, sc in sp **before** next dc, skip next 2 dc, 5 dc in sp **before** next dc, skip next 2 dc, sc in sp **before** next dc; join with slip st to first dc, finish off.

Size Medium Only

Turn; slip st in sp **before** next dc, ch 3, 4 dc in same sp, ★ (skip next 2 dc, sc in sp **before** next dc, skip next 2 dc, 5 dc in sp **before** next dc) across to within 2 dc of next ch-2 sp, skip next dc, sc in next dc, 5 dc in next ch-2 sp, sc in next dc, skip next dc, 5 dc in sp **before** next dc; repeat from ★ once **more**, skip next 2 dc, sc in sp **before** next dc, skip next 2 dc, 5 dc in sp **before** next dc, skip next 2 dc, sc in sp **before** next dc; join with slip st to first dc, finish off.

---

2. Best Little Hunting Buddy

EASY

Shown on page 5.

Size	Chest Measurement
X-Small	12" (30.5 cm)
Small	16" (40.5 cm)
Medium	20" (51 cm)
Large	24" (61 cm)

Size Note: Instructions are written for size X-Small with sizes Small, Medium, and Large in braces { }. Instructions will be easier to read if you circle all the numbers pertaining to your dog's size. If only one number is given, it applies to all sizes.

MATERIALS

Medium Weight Yarn
[7 ounces, 364 yards (198 grams, 333 meters) per skein]: 1 skein
Crochet hook, size I (5.5 mm) **or** size needed for gauge
1" (26 mm) Button - 1
Sewing needle and thread

GAUGE: 12 dc and 7 rows = 4" (10 cm)

Gauge Swatch: 4" (10 cm) square
Ch 14.
Row 1: Dc in fourth ch from hook **(3 skipped chs count as first dc)** and in each ch across: 12 dc.
Rows 2-7: Ch 3 **(counts as first dc)**, turn; dc in next dc and in each dc across.
Finish off.

Instructions begin on page 4.

STITCH GUIDE

BEGINNING DECREASE (uses first 2 dc)
Ch 2, turn; dc in next dc **(counts as one dc)**.
DECREASE (uses next 2 dc)
★ YO, insert hook in **next** dc, YO and pull up a loop, YO and draw through 2 loops on hook; repeat from ★ once **more**, YO and draw through all 3 loops on hook **(counts as one dc)**.

RIBBING

Ch 11{13-15-17}.

Row 1: Sc in second ch from hook and in each ch across: 10{12-14-16} sc.

Rows 2 thru 26{32-40-44}: Ch 1, turn; sc in Back Loop Only of each sc across *(Fig. 1, page 18)*.

Joining Rnd: Ch 1, turn; working in Back Loops Only of sc on last row **and** in free loops of beginning ch *(Fig. 3, page 19)*, slip st in each st across; do **not** finish off.

BODY

Row 1 (Right side)**:** Ch 3 **(counts as first dc, now and throughout)**, do **not** turn; dc in end of next 23{29-37-41} rows, leave remaining 2 rows unworked: 24{30-38-42} dc.

Note: Loop a short piece of yarn around any stitch to mark Row 1 as **right** side.

Rows 2 thru 8{9-10-12}: Ch 3, turn; dc in next dc and in each dc across.

Row 9{10-11-13}: Work beginning decrease, dc in next dc and in each dc across to last 2 dc, decrease: 22{28-36-40} dc.

Next Row: Ch 3, turn; dc in next dc and in each dc across.

Decrease Row: Work beginning decrease, dc in next dc and in each dc across to last 2 dc, decrease: 20{26-34-38} dc.

Repeat last 2 rows, 2{2-3-3} times: 16{22-28-32} dc.

Finish off.

TUMMY STRAP

Row 1: With **right** side facing, join yarn with slip st in end of 5th{6th-7th-8th} row on Body; ch 3, dc in end of next 4{4-6-8} rows: 5{5-7-9} dc.

Rows 2 thru 9{10-12-13}: Ch 3, turn; dc in next dc and in each dc across.

Row 10{11-13-14} (Buttonhole row)**:** Ch 3, turn; dc in next 1{1-2-3} dc, ch 1, skip next dc (buttonhole made), dc in last 2{2-3-4} dc: 4{4-6-8} dc and one ch-1 sp.

Row 11{12-14-15}: Ch 3, turn; dc in next 1{1-2-3} dc, dc in next ch-1 sp and in last 2{2-3-4} dc: 5{5-7-9} dc.

Row 12{13-15-16}: Ch 3, turn; dc in next dc and in each dc across.

Row 13{14-16-17} (Buttonhole row)**:** Ch 3, turn; dc in next 1{1-2-3} dc, ch 1, skip next dc (buttonhole made), dc in last 2{2-3-4} dc: 4{4-6-8} dc and one ch-1 sp.

Row 14{15-17-18}: Ch 3, turn; dc in next 1{1-2-3} dc, dc in next ch-1 sp and in last 2{2-3-4} dc; finish off.

Sew button to center back of Body.

3. Glamour Gal

EASY

Shown on Back Cover.

Size	Chest Measurement
X-Small	12" (30.5 cm)
Small	16" (40.5 cm)
Medium	20" (51 cm)
Large	24" (61 cm)

Size Note: Instructions are written for size X-Small with sizes Small, Medium, and Large in braces { }. Instructions will be easier to read if you circle all the numbers pertaining to your dog's size. If only one number is given, it applies to all sizes.

MATERIALS

Bulky Weight Yarn
[1$^3/_4$ ounces, 82 yards (50 grams, 75 meters) per skein]: 1{1-2-3} skein(s)
Crochet hook, size I (5.5 mm) **or** size needed for gauge
1" (26 mm) Button - 1
Sewing needle and thread

GAUGE: 12 dc and 7 rows = 4" (10 cm)

Gauge Swatch: 4" (10 cm) square
Ch 14.
Row 1: Dc in fourth ch from hook **(3 skipped chs count as first dc)** and in each ch across: 12 dc.
Rows 2-7: Ch 3 **(counts as first dc)**, turn; dc in next dc and in each dc across.
Finish off.

STITCH GUIDE

BEGINNING DECREASE (uses first 2 dc)
Ch 2, turn; dc in next dc **(counts as one dc)**.
DECREASE (uses next 2 dc)
★ YO, insert hook in **next** dc, YO and pull up a loop, YO and draw through 2 loops on hook; repeat from ★ once **more**, YO and draw through all 3 loops on hook **(counts as one dc)**.

RIBBING

Ch 9{11-13-15}.

Row 1: Sc in second ch from hook and in each ch across: 8{10-12-14} sc.

Rows 2 thru 24{28-32-36}: Ch 1, turn; sc in Back Loop Only of each sc across *(Fig. 1, page 18)*.

Joining Row: Ch 1, turn; working in Back Loops Only of sc on last row **and** in free loops of beginning ch *(Fig. 3, page 19)*, slip st in each st across; do **not** finish off.

BODY

Row 1 (Right side)**:** Ch 3 **(counts as first dc, now and throughout)**, do **not** turn; dc in end of next 21{25-29-33} rows, leave remaining 2 rows unworked: 22{26-30-34} dc.

Note: Loop a short piece of yarn around any stitch to mark Row 1 as **right** side.

Rows 2 thru 3{5-7-9}: Ch 3, turn; dc in next dc and in each dc across.

Row 4{6-8-10}: Ch 3, turn; dc in next 3{4-5-6} dc, ★ 2 dc in next dc, dc in next 5{6-7-8} dc; repeat from ★ across: 25{29-33-37} dc.

Rows 5{7-9-11} thru 9{11-13-15}: Ch 3, turn; dc in next dc and in each dc across.

Rows 10{12-14-16} thru 13{17-19-23}: Work beginning decrease, dc in next dc and in each dc across last 2 dc, decrease: 17{17-21-21} dc.

Ruffle Edging: Ch 1, do **not** turn; sc in same st, ch 3, (sc, ch 3) evenly spaced around entire sweater; join with slip st to first sc, finish off.

TUMMY STRAP

Ch 7{7-9-9}.

Row 1: Dc in fourth ch from hook **(3 skipped chs count as first dc)** and in each ch across: 5{5-7-7} dc.

Rows 2 thru 9{11-13-15}: Ch 3, turn; dc in next dc and in each dc across.

Row 10{12-14-16} (Buttonhole row)**:** Ch 3, turn; dc in next 1{1-2-2} dc, ch 1, skip next dc (buttonhole made), dc in last 2{2-3-3} dc: 4{4-6-6} dc and one ch-1 sp.

Row 11{13-15-17}: Ch 3, turn; dc in next 1{1-2-2} dc, dc in next ch-1 sp and in last 2{2-3-3} dc: 5{5-7-7} dc.

Row 12{14-16-18}: Ch 3, turn; dc in next dc and in each dc across.

Row 13{15-17-19} (Buttonhole row)**:** Ch 3, turn; dc in next 1{1-2-2} dc, ch 1, skip next dc (buttonhole made), dc in last 2{2-3-3} dc: 4{4-6-6} dc and one ch-1 sp.

Row 14{16-18-20}: Ch 1, turn; sc in first dc, (ch 3, sc in next st) across; finish off.

Sew side of Tummy Strap under ruffle on left edge of Body, beginning 5{5-6-6} rows down from Ribbing.

Sew button to center back of Body.

---

4. Santa's Best Helper

INTERMEDIATE

Shown on page 8.

Size	Chest Measurement
X-Small	12" (30.5 cm)
Small	16" (40.5 cm)
Medium	20" (51 cm)
Large	24" (61 cm)

Size Note: Instructions are written for size X-Small with sizes Small, Medium, and Large in braces { }. Instructions will be easier to read if you circle all the numbers pertaining to your dog's size. If only one number is given, it applies to all sizes.

MATERIALS

MEDIUM 4

Medium Weight Yarn
[3 ounces, 170 yards
(85 grams, 155 meters) per skein]:
Red - 1{1-1-2} skein(s)
Black - 1 skein

SUPER BULKY 6

Super Bulky Weight Yarn
[6 ounces, 140 yards
(170 grams, 128 meters) per skein]:
White - 1 skein
Crochet hook, size I (5.5 mm) **or** size needed for gauge
Gold metallic cord - small amount
Yarn needle
Sewing needle and thread
1" (26 mm) Button - 1

GAUGE: 13 sc and 16 rows = 4" (10 cm)

Gauge Swatch: 4" (10 cm) square
With Red, ch 14.
Row 1: Sc in second ch from hook and in each ch across: 13 sc.
Rows 2-16: Ch 1, turn; sc in each sc across.
Finish off.

STITCH GUIDE

BEGINNING DECREASE (uses first 2 sc)
Pull up a loop in first 2 sc, YO and draw through all 3 loops on hook **(counts as one sc)**.
DECREASE (uses next 2 sc)
Pull up a loop in next 2 sc, YO and draw through all 3 loops on hook **(counts as one sc)**.

Instructions begin on page 10.

4

5

RIBBING

With Red, ch 9{11-13-15}.

Row 1: Sc in second ch from hook and in each ch across: 8{10-12-14} sc.

Rows 2 thru 20{30-40-50}: Ch 1, turn; sc in Back Loop Only of each sc across *(Fig. 1, page 18)*.

Joining Row: Ch 1, turn; working in Back Loops Only of sc on last row **and** in free loops of beginning ch *(Fig. 3, page 19)*, slip st in each st across; do **not** finish off.

BODY

Rnd 1 (Right side)**:** Ch 1, do **not** turn; work 38{48-58-68} sc evenly spaced in end of rows around; join with slip st to first sc.

Note: Loop a short piece of yarn around any stitch to mark Rnd 1 as **right** side.

Rnds 2 thru 8{12-18-24}: Ch 1, turn; sc in same st and in each sc around; join with slip st to first sc.

Begin working in rows.

Row 1: Ch 1, turn; sc in next 20{30-40-50} sc, leave remaining 18 sc unworked.

Rows 2 thru 9{11-13-15}: Ch 1, turn; sc in each sc across; at end of last row, change to Black in last sc made *(Fig. 2, page 18)*.

BELT

Rows 1 thru 6{6-8-8}: Ch 1, turn; sc in each sc across; at the end of last row, change to Red in last sc made.

BOTTOM

Rows 1 thru 6{6-8-8}: Ch 1, turn; sc in each sc across.

Decrease Row: Ch 1, turn; work beginning decrease, sc in each sc across to last 2 sc, decrease: 18{28-38-48} sc.

Next Row: Ch 1, turn; sc in each sc across.

Repeat last 2 rows twice: 14{24-34-44} sc.

Finish off.

Fur Trim: With **right** side facing, join White with slip st in any st; ch 1, sc evenly around entire sweater; join with slip st to first sc, finish off.

Neck Trim: With **right** side facing, join White with slip st in end of any row of Ribbing; ch 1, sc evenly around; join with slip st to first sc, finish off.

TUMMY STRAP

With Black, ch 7{7-9-9}.

Row 1: Dc in fourth ch from hook **(3 skipped chs count as first dc)** and in each ch across: 5{5-7-7} dc.

Rows 2 thru 6{7-8-9}: Ch 3 **(counts as first dc, now and throughout)**, turn; dc in next dc and in each dc across.

Row 7{8-9-10} (Buttonhole row)**:** Ch 3, turn; dc in next 1{1-2-2} dc, ch 1, skip next dc (buttonhole made), dc in last 2{2-3-3} dc: 4{4-6-6} dc and one ch-1 sp.

Row 8{9-10-11}: Ch 1, turn; sc in first 2{2-3-3} dc, sc in next ch-1 sp and in last 2{2-3-3} dc; finish off.

Sew Tummy Strap to **wrong** side of left edge on Body along Belt rows.

Sew button to wrong side of Body on opposite edge.

Using photo as a guide for placement, thread yarn needle with an 18" (45.5 cm) length of Gold cord and stitch a buckle on center of Belt.

5. Patriotic Pup

INTERMEDIATE

Shown on page 9.

Size	Chest Measurement
X-Small	12" (30.5 cm)
Small	16" (40.5 cm)
Medium	20" (51 cm)
Large	24" (61 cm)

Size Note: Instructions are written for size X-Small with sizes Small, Medium, and Large in braces { }. Instructions will be easier to read if you circle all the numbers pertaining to your dog's size. If only one number is given, it applies to all sizes.

MATERIALS

MEDIUM 4

Worsted Weight Yarn
[3 1/2 ounces, 198 yards
(100 grams, 181 meters) per skein]:
Red - 1{1-2-3} skein(s)
White - 1{1-2-3} skein(s)
Blue - 1{1-2-3} skein(s)
Crochet hook, size I (5.5 mm) **or** size needed for gauge
Yarn needle
Sewing needle and thread
1" (26 mm) Star button - 1
Small liberty bell - 1

GAUGE: 12 dc and 7 rows = 4" (10 cm)

Gauge Swatch: 4" (10 cm) square
Ch 14.
Row 1: Dc in fourth ch from hook **(3 skipped chs count as first dc)** and in each ch across: 12 dc.
Rows 2-7: Ch 3 **(counts as first dc)**, turn; dc in next dc and in each dc across.
Finish off.

STITCH GUIDE

BEGINNING DECREASE (uses first 2 dc)
Ch 2, turn; dc in next dc **(counts as one dc)**.
DECREASE (uses next 2 dc)
★ YO, insert hook in **next** dc, YO and pull up a loop, YO and draw through 2 loops on hook; repeat from ★ once **more**, YO and draw through all 3 loops on hook **(counts as one dc)**.

RIBBING

With Blue and leaving a long end for sewing, ch 9{11-13-15}.

Row 1: Sc in second ch from hook and in each ch across: 8{10-12-14} sc.

Rows 2 thru 26{30-40-50}: Ch 1, turn; sc in Back Loop Only of each sc across *(Fig. 1, page 18)*; at end of last row, change to White in last sc made *(Fig. 2, page 18)*.

BODY

Stripe Sequence
Alternate 2 rows of White and 2 rows of Red throughout.

Row 1 (Right side)**:** Ch 3, do **not** turn; working in end of rows, dc in same row, ★ dc in next 2{1-1-1} row(s), 2 dc in next row; repeat from ★ 4{6-10-13} times **more**, dc in next 0{3-1-0} row(s) *(see Zeros, page 18)*, 2 dc in next 0{0-0-1} row(s), leave remaining 10{12-16-20} rows unworked: 22{26-36-46} dc.

Row 2: Ch 3, turn; dc in next dc and in each dc across, changing to Red in last dc made.

Rows 3 thru 12{14-16-18}: Ch 3, turn; dc in next dc and in each dc across.

Instructions continued on page 14.

6

1
7

Decrease Row: Work beginning decrease, dc in next dc and in each dc across to last 2 dc, decrease: 20{24-34-44} dc.

Next Row: Ch 3, turn; dc in next dc and in each dc across.

Repeat last 2 rows once: 18{22-32-42} dc.

Finish off.

Edging: With **right** side facing and working in end of rows on Body, join Red with sc in first row *(see Joining With Sc, page 18)*; sc evenly across to last row, 3 sc in first dc, sc in each dc across to last dc, 3 sc in last dc; sc evenly across end of rows on Body; finish off.

Thread yarn needle with long end and sew Ribbing seam, matching sc on last row to free loops of beginning ch *(Fig. 3, page 19)*.

TUMMY STRAP

Row 1: With **right** side facing and Ribbing to the left, join Red with dc in sc on Edging 6{7-8$^1/_2$-10}"/15{18-21.5-25.5} cm down from Ribbing *(see Joining With Dc, page 18)*; dc in next 4{4-6-8} sc: 5{5-7-9} dc.

Rows 2 thru 5{8-11-14}: Ch 3, dc in next dc and in each dc across.

Row 6{9-12-15} (Buttonhole row)**:** Ch 3, turn; dc in next 1{1-2-3} dc, ch 1, skip next dc (buttonhole made), dc in last 2{2-3-4} dc: 4{4-6-8} dc and one ch-1 sps.

Row 7{10-13-16}: Ch 3, turn; dc in next 1{1-2-3} dc, dc in next ch-1 sp and in last 2{2-3-4} dc: 5{5-7-9} dc.

Row 8{11-14-17}: Ch 3, turn; dc in next dc and in each dc across.

Rows 9{12-15-18} and 10{13-16-19}: Repeat Rows 6{9-12-15} and 7{10-13-16}.

Finish off.

Sew button to opposite edge of Body.
Sew bell to Ribbing at center front of neck.

---

6. Rainbow Jacket

INTERMEDIATE

Shown on page 12.

Size	**Chest Measurement**
Small/Medium	20" (51 cm)
Large/X-Large	24" (61 cm)

Size Note: Instructions are written for size Small/Medium with size Large/X-Large in braces { }. Instructions will be easier to read if you circle all the numbers pertaining to your dog's size. If only one number is given, it applies to all sizes.

MATERIALS

MEDIUM 4

Medium Weight Yarn
[7 ounces, 364 yards
(198 grams, 333 meters) per skein]:
Black - 1 skein
Scrap Colors - 100 yards (91 meters)
Crochet hook, size I (5.5 mm) **or** size needed for gauge
Yarn needle
Sewing needle and thread
1" (26 mm) Button - 1

GAUGE SWATCH: 3$^1/_2$" (9 cm) square
Work same as Square.

SQUARE [Make 11{14}]

With first scrap color, ch 4; join with slip st to form a ring.

Rnd 1 (Right side)**:** Ch 3 **(counts as first dc, now and throughout)**, 2 dc in ring, ch 2, (3 dc in ring, ch 2) 3 times; join with slip st to first dc, finish off: 12 dc and 4 ch-2 sps.

Note: Loop a short piece of yarn around any stitch to mark Rnd 1 as **right** side.

Rnd 2: With **wrong** side facing, join next color with dc in any ch-2 sp *(see Joining With Dc, page 18)*; (2 dc, ch 2, 3 dc) in same sp, ch 1, ★ (3 dc, ch 2, 3 dc) in next ch-2 sp, ch 1; repeat from ★ 2 times **more**; join with slip st to first dc, finish off: 24 dc and 8 sps.

Rnd 3: With **right** side facing, join Black with dc in any ch-2 sp; (2 dc, ch 2, 3 dc) in same sp, ch 1, 3 dc in next ch-1 sp, ★ (3 dc, ch 2, 3 dc) in next ch-2 sp, ch 1, 3 dc in next ch-1 sp, ch 1; repeat from ★ 2 times **more**; join with slip st to first dc, finish off.

ASSEMBLY

Using diagram as a guide for placement, with Black and working in **both** loops of **both** pieces, whipstitch Squares together *(Fig. 5, page 19)*, beginning in second ch of first corner ch-2 and ending in first ch of second corner ch-2, forming 3{4} vertical strips of 3 Squares each; then whipstitch strips together in same manner. Whipstitch remaining two Squares together in same manner to form Tummy Strap, then whipstitch to center left edge Square.

Diagram

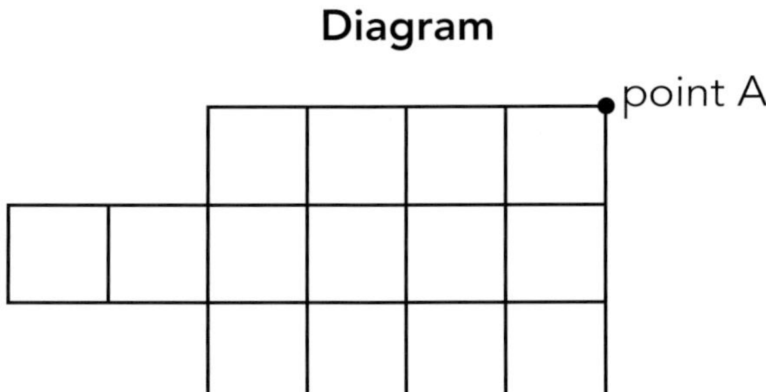

RIBBING

With **right** side facing, skip first corner ch-2 sp (point A) and join Black with slip st in next ch-1 sp, ch 8.

Row 1: Sc in second ch from hook and in each ch across, slip st in next dc: 8 sts.

Row 2: Ch 1, turn; skip first slip st, sc in Back Loop Only of each sc across *(Fig. 1, page 18)*: 7 sc.

Row 3: Ch 1, turn; sc in Back Loop Only of each sc across, slip st in next dc: 8 sts.

Rows 4-10: Repeat Rows 2 and 3, 3 times; then repeat Row 2 once **more**.

Row 11: Ch 1, turn; sc in Back Loop Only of each sc across, slip st in next joining: 8 sts.

Rows 12-28: Repeat Rows 2 and 3, 8 times; then repeat Row 2 once **more**.

Repeat Rows 11-28, 0{1} time(s) *(see Zeros, page 18)*; then repeat Rows 11-22 once **more**.

Last Row: Ch 1, turn; sc in each sc across, slip st in last ch-1 sp; finish off leaving a long end for sewing.

Thread yarn needle with long end and sew Ribbing seam, matching sc on last row to free loops of beginning ch *(Fig. 3, page 19)*.

Using corner ch-2 sps on Tummy Strap Square as buttonholes, sew buttons to opposite edge of Body.

7. Canine Comfort

EASY

Shown on page 13 & Front Cover.

MATERIALS

BULKY 5

Bulky Weight Yarn
[6 ounces, 185 yards
(170 grams, 169 meters) per skein]: 1 skein
Crochet hook, size K (6.5 mm) **or** size needed for gauge

GAUGE: In pattern, 8 dc = 3 3/4" (9.5 cm);
5 rows = 3" (7.5 cm)

Gauge Swatch: 4 1/4"w x 3"h
(10.75 cm x 7.5 cm)
Ch 13.
Work same as Body for 5 rows.
Finish off.

BODY

Ch 33, place marker in third ch from hook for st placement.

Row 1: Dc in fourth ch from hook **(3 skipped chs count as first dc)** and in each ch across: 31 dc.

Row 2 (Right side)**:** Ch 3 **(counts as first dc, now and throughout)**, turn; (skip next dc, 2 dc in next dc) across to last 2 dc, skip next dc, dc in last dc: 30 dc.

Row 3: Ch 3, turn; dc in same st, ★ skip next 2 dc, 2 dc in sp **before** next dc *(Fig. 4, page 19)*; repeat from ★ across to last dc, dc in last dc: 31 dc.

Rows 4-22: Ch 3, turn; dc in same st, (skip next 2 dc, 2 dc in sp **before** next dc) across to last 2 dc, skip next dc, dc in last dc.

Row 23: Ch 3, turn; dc in next dc and in each dc across; do **not** finish off.

EDGING

Ch 3, turn; 4 dc in same st, skip next 2 dc, sc in next dc, (skip next dc, 5 dc in next dc, skip next dc, sc in next dc) across to last 3 dc, skip next 2 dc, 5 dc in last dc; † working in end of rows, sc in first row, (5 dc in next row, sc in next row) across †; working in free loops of beginning ch *(Fig. 3, page 19)*, 5 dc in marked ch, skip next 2 chs, sc in next ch, (skip next ch, 5 dc in next ch, skip next ch, sc in next ch) across to last 3 chs, skip next 2 chs, 5 dc in last ch; repeat from † to † once; join with slip st to first dc, finish off.

General Instructions

ABBREVIATIONS

ch(s) chain(s)
cm centimeters
dc double crochet(s)
mm millimeters
Rnd(s) Round(s)
sc single crochet(s)
sp(s) space(s)
st(s) stitch(es)
YO yarn over

★ — work instructions following ★ as many **more** times as indicated in addition to the first time.

† to † — work all instructions from first † to second † **as many** times as specified.

( ) or **[ ]** — work enclosed instructions **as many** times as specified by the number immediately following **or** work all enclosed instructions in the stitch or space indicated **or** contains explanatory remarks.

colon (:) — the number(s) given after a colon at the end of a row or round denote(s) the number of stitches you should have on that row or round.

Yarn Weight Symbol & Names	SUPER FINE 1	FINE 2	LIGHT 3	MEDIUM 4	BULKY 5	SUPER BULKY 6
Type of Yarns in Category	Sock, Fingering Baby	Sport, Baby	DK, Light Worsted	Worsted, Afghan, Aran	Chunky, Craft, Rug	Bulky, Roving
Crochet Gauge Ranges in Single Crochet to 4" (10 cm)	21-32 sts	16-20 sts	12-17 sts	11-14 sts	8-11 sts	5-9 sts
Advised Hook Size Range	B-1 to E-4	E-4 to 7	7 to I-9	I-9 to K-10.5	K-10.5 to M-13	M-13 and larger

CROCHET TERMINOLOGY		
UNITED STATES		**INTERNATIONAL**
slip stitch (slip st)	=	single crochet (sc)
single crochet (sc)	=	double crochet (dc)
half double crochet (hdc)	=	half treble crochet (htr)
double crochet (dc)	=	treble crochet (tr)
treble crochet (tr)	=	double treble crochet (dtr)
double treble crochet (dtr)	=	triple treble crochet (ttr)
triple treble crochet (tr tr)	=	quadruple treble crochet (qtr)
skip	=	miss

CROCHET HOOKS													
U.S.	B-1	C-2	D-3	E-4	F-5	G-6	H-8	I-9	J-10	K-10½	N	P	Q
Metric - mm	2.25	2.75	3.25	3.5	3.75	4	5	5.5	6	6.5	9	10	15

BEGINNER	Projects for first-time crocheters using basic stitches. Minimal shaping.
EASY	Projects using yarn with basic stitches, repetitive stitch patterns, simple color changes, and simple shaping and finishing.
INTERMEDIATE	Projects using a variety of techniques, such as basic lace patterns or color patterns, mid-level shaping and finishing.
EXPERIENCED	Projects with intricate stitch patterns, techniques and dimension, such as non-repeating patterns, multi-color techniques, fine threads, small hooks, detailed shaping and refined finishing.

GAUGE

Exact gauge is **essential** for proper size. Before beginning your project, make the sample swatch given in the individual instructions in the yarn and hook specified. After completing the swatch, measure it, counting your stitches and rows or rounds carefully. If your swatch is larger or smaller than specified, **make another, changing hook size to get the correct gauge**. Keep trying until you find the size hook that will give you the specified gauge.

HINTS

Make a habit of taking care of loose ends as you work. Thread a yarn needle with the yarn end. With **wrong** side facing, weave the needle through several stitches, then reverse the direction and weave it back through several stitches. When ends are secure, clip them off close to work.

ZEROS

To consolidate the length of an involved pattern, Zeros are sometimes used so that all sizes can be combined. For example, dc in next 0{2-1-0} rows means the Small size would dc in next 2 rows, the Medium size would dc in next row, and the X-Small and Large size would do nothing.

JOINING WITH SC

When instructed to join with sc, begin with a slip knot on hook. Insert hook in stitch or space indicated, YO and pull up a loop, YO and draw through both loops on hook.

JOINING WITH DC

When instructed to join with dc, begin with a slip knot on hook. YO, holding loop on hook, insert hook in stitch or space indicated, YO and pull up a loop (3 loops on hook), (YO and draw through 2 loops on hook) twice.

BACK LOOP ONLY

Work only in loop(s) indicated by arrow *(Fig. 1)*.

Fig. 1

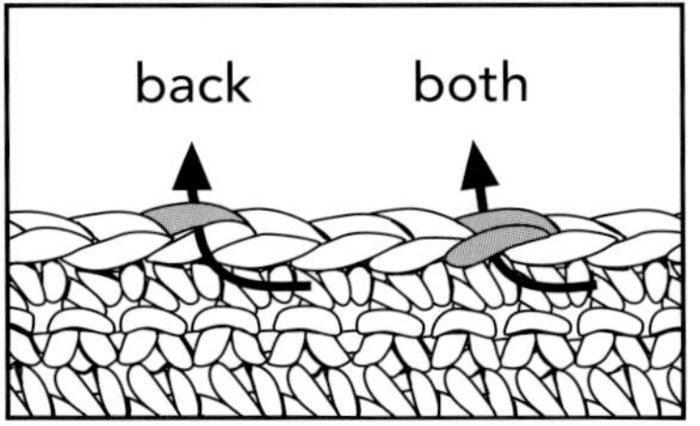

CHANGING COLORS

Work the last stitch to within one step of completion, hook new yarn *(Fig. 2)* and draw through all loops on hook. Cut old yarn and work over both ends.

Fig. 2

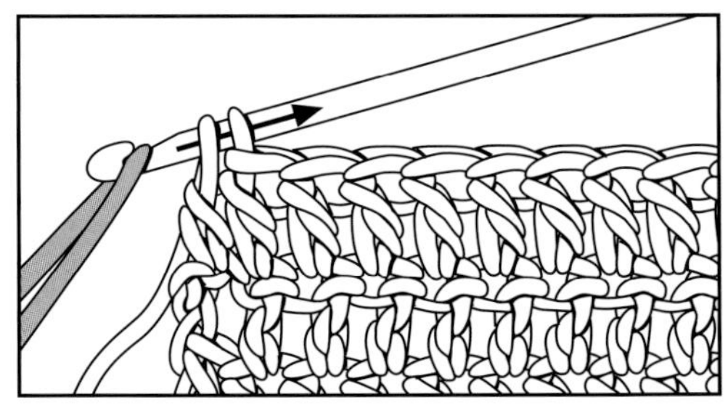

FREE LOOPS OF A CHAIN

When instructed to work in free loops of a chain, work in loop indicated by arrow *(Fig. 3)*.

Fig. 3

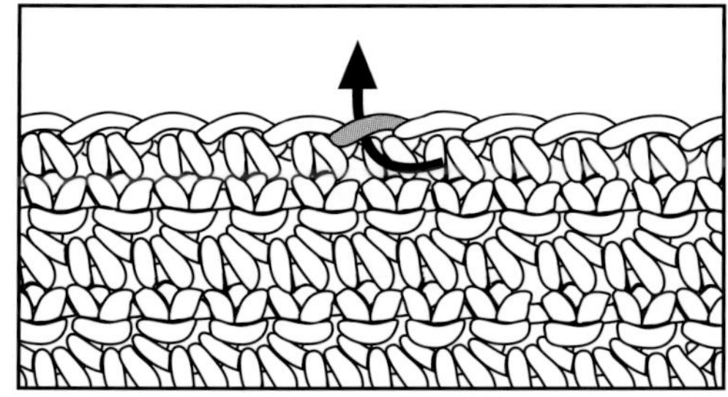

WORKING IN SPACE BEFORE A STITCH

When instructed to work in space **before** a stitch or in spaces **between** stitches, insert hook in space indicated by arrow *(Fig. 4)*.

Fig. 4

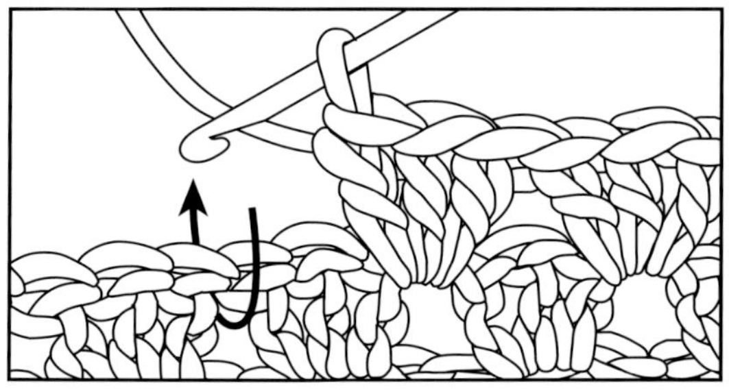

WHIPSTITCH

Place two Squares or Strips with **wrong** sides together. Beginning in second ch of first corner ch-2 and ending in first ch of next corner ch-2, sew through both pieces once to secure the beginning of the seam, leaving an ample yarn end to weave in later. Insert the needle from **front** to **back** through **both** loops on **both** pieces *(Fig. 5)*. Bring the needle around and insert it from **front** to **back** through next loops of both pieces. Continue in this manner across to next corner, keeping the sewing yarn fairly loose.

Fig. 5

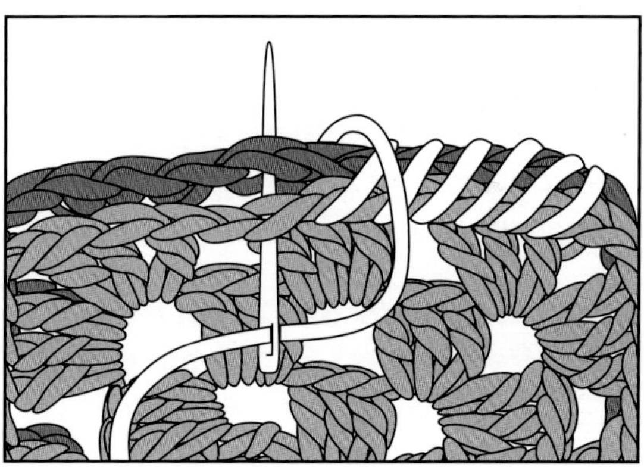

YARN INFORMATION

Each item in this leaflet was made with Medium, Bulky, or Super Bulky Weight Yarn. Any brand of specific weight yarn may be used. It is best to refer to the yardage/meters when determining how many ball or skeins to purchase. Remember, to arrive at the finished size, it is the GAUGE/TENSION that is important, not the brand of yarn.

For your convenience, listed below are colors used to create our photography models.

1. PEDIGREED PONCHO
Lion Brand® Homespun®
#301 Shaker

2. BEST LITTLE HUNTING BUDDY
Red Heart® Super Saver®
#971 Camouflage

3. GLAMOUR GAL
Lion Brand® Moonlight Mohair
#203 Safari

4. SANTA'S BEST HELPER
Red Heart® Super Saver®
Red - #319 Cherry Red
Black - #312 Black
Red Heart® Baby Clouds™
White - #9311 White

5. PATRIOTIC PUP
Red Heart® Classic®
Red - #902 Jockey Red
White - #1 White
Blue - #848 Skipper Blue

6. RAINBOW JACKET
Red Heart® Super Saver®
Black - #312 Black
Scrap Colors

7. CANINE COMFORT
Lion Brand® Homespun®
#301 Shaker

We have made every effort to ensure that these instructions are accurate and complete. We cannot, however, be responsible for human error, typographical mistakes, or variations in individual work.

Production Team: Technical Editor - Lois J. Long; Editorial Writer - Susan McManus Johnson; Artist - Ashley Carozza; Senior Artist - Lora Puls; Photo Stylist - Cassie Francioni; and - Photographer Jason Masters.